Pilates for Dogs

(those special dogs that really care)

Meet the teacher

This is an
utterly silly book
BUT
an utterly TRUE account!
Ladies: take note!
(gentlemen too)

Pilates for Dogs

Illustrated by Kath Walker

MQP

Introduction

The reason many of us find Pilates so irresistible is that it is a form of exercise that is accessible to anyone, regardless of level of fitness, age or size. With regular practice it has the ability to make you feel fitter, stronger, more flexible, leaner. After even a few sessions most people notice an improvement in their breathing, balance, co-ordination, poise and general well-being – both when exercising and as they go about their daily activities.

Although this book takes a somewhat lighthearted approach to the Pilates method, this is from a place of the deepest respect for the system, and is in no way intended as a sleight on what is one of the best, most effective exercise techniques in existence, one that draws on a variety of sources from ancient eastern to western practices alike.

No one, I hope, will be crazy enough to attempt to take their faithful furry friend through any of the movements shown here. That would be to entirely miss the point of this book, which is to inspire you not to release your pooch's Pilates potential, but rather to allow you to get in touch with your own inner puppy.

...Meet the girls...

Alicia

Jessica

Showstopper

Fashion queen

Bella

Lily

Loves housework

Doesn't love it

So...on one fine day we find a clear cut case of...

Doggie
Doldrums!

So...they get together to figure out what in the world the should do...Do they:

A: Really want to change there lives? i.e.suffer to get fit and beautiful?

B: Go out and shuffle through some really good trash?

C. Go out and get the best bone money can buy...?!

And...the answer...

...Pilates!

...So off they scamper...

...ah, the *abdominal core*...*squeeze that pelvis, squish those abs*...

...and *hip openings!*...

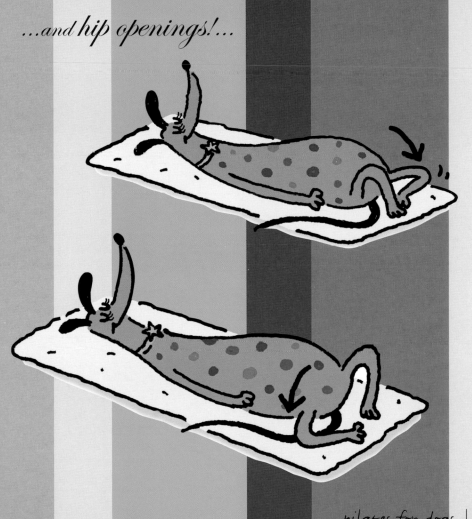

Raise girls...

yip yip hooray!

...and now for zee dreaded **hundreds**...

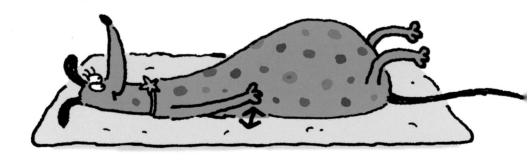

*Now for some **neck pulls** ladies...*

...***boring!***...mental note to self...paws: (pause ha ha...

Q: What has got four legs and an arm?

A: A Rottweiler in a playground! hee hee

Now curl ladies...

Q: What dog loves to take bubble baths?
A: A shampoodle!

...got it!...You can learn a lot from a dog: obedience, loyalty, and the importance of turning around three times before lying down...(take note readers!)

Now double leg lift...

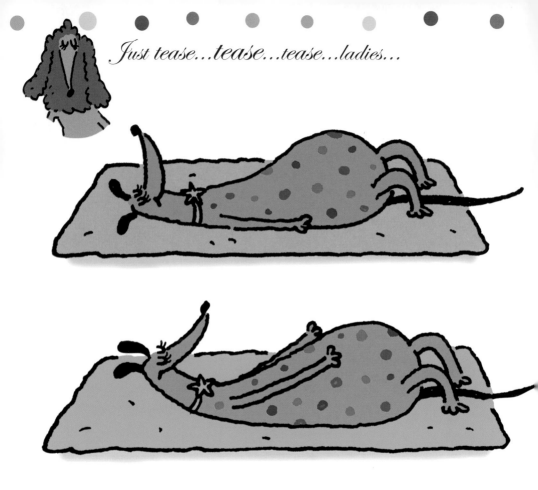

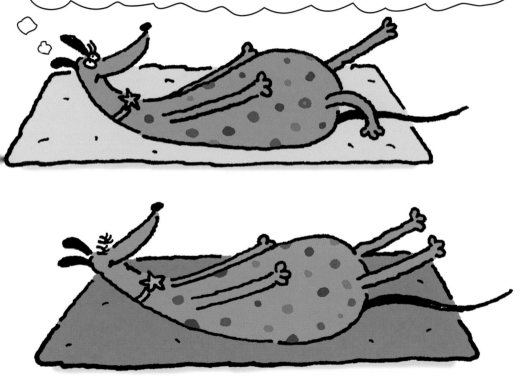

Roll up...

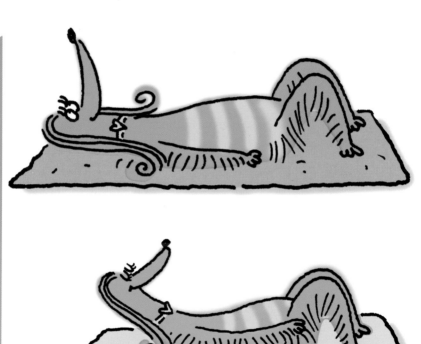

...in every way, every day I'm getting better and better ooo ah!

hoo haa hee hee toodle dee poodle dah dee!

...and now for the big roll over...

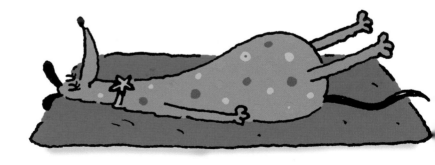

Now for the dart ...

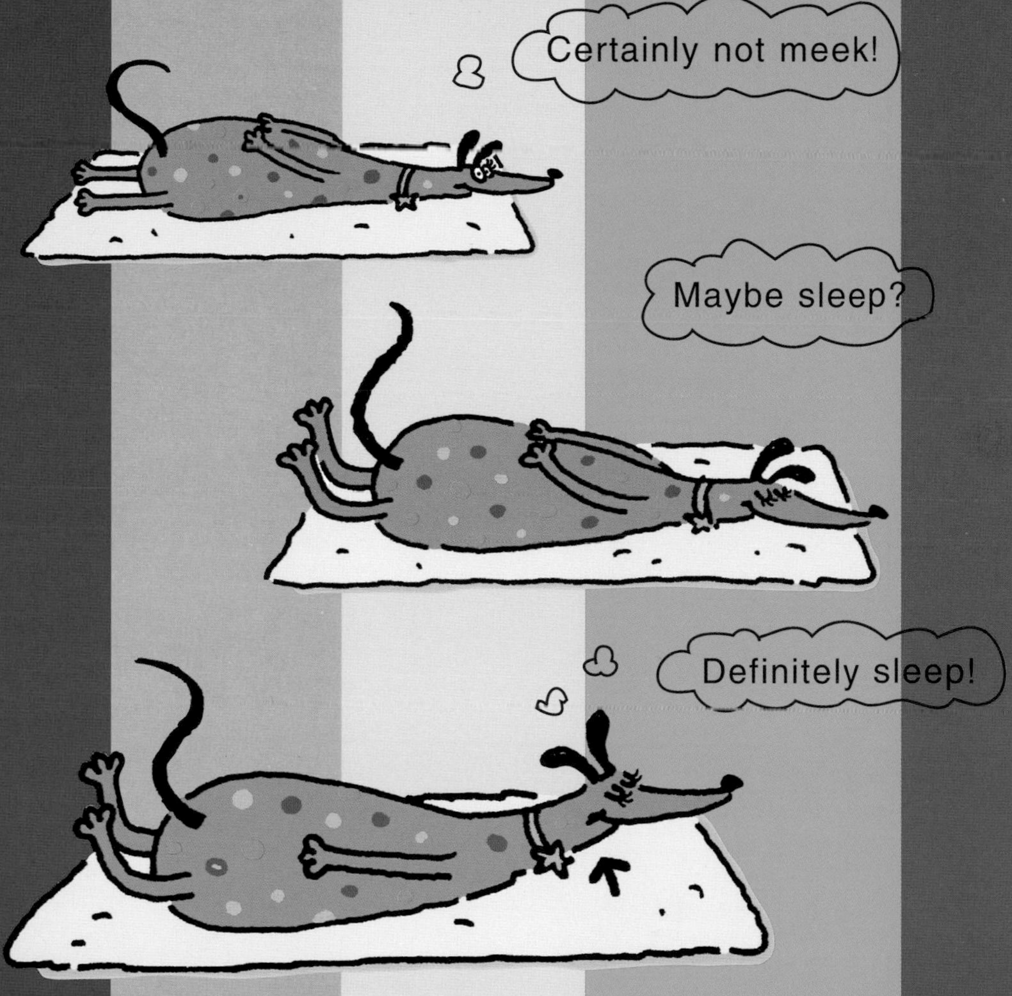
Certainly not meek!
Maybe sleep?
Definitely sleep!

So...where **does** she get her hair done?

Single leg stretch ladies...just do what I do! Yes?

Double leg stretch girls...

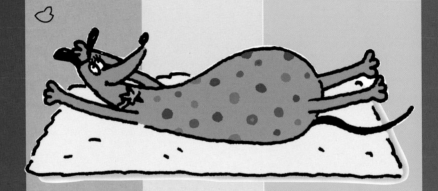

I don't care where she gets her hair done... it's obviously **not** natural.

Shoulder lifts ladies...

Shoulder raises...

...my paws hurt!

...side bends ...

and the hamstring stretch...

...hamstring eh – I'm thinking **hambone**!

Now for the cat position…

The chest stretch...

Now for some squats against the wall ladies...

pilates for dogs | 73

Abdominal stretches...

Oohh!

Oooohhh

Three months later the **Va Va Voom**
factor has definitely kicked in...

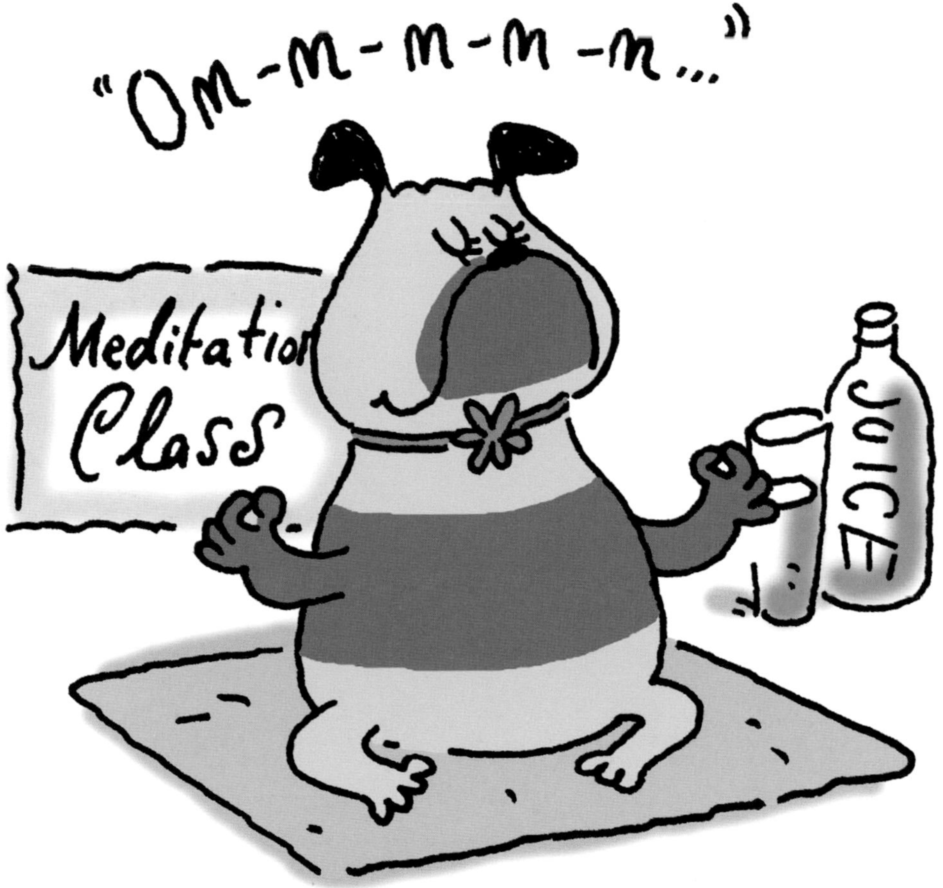
"Om-m-m-m-m..."
Meditation Class
JUICE

...the let's go **healthy** facto
has definitely kicked in...

Published by MQ Publications Limited
12 The Ivories, 6–8 Northampton Street
London N1 2HY
Tel: +44 (0) 20 7359 2244
Fax:+44 (0) 20 7359 1616
email: mail@mqpublications.com
website: www.mqpublications.com

ISBN: 1-84072-608-3
10 9 8 7 6 5 4 3 2 1

Printed and bound in China